PRAISE My Pet!

ADULT COLORING BOOK

WWW.PRAISEMYPET.COM

Color Johnny and Marlee!

Color Del!

Color Jager!

Color Roscoe and Peanut!

7

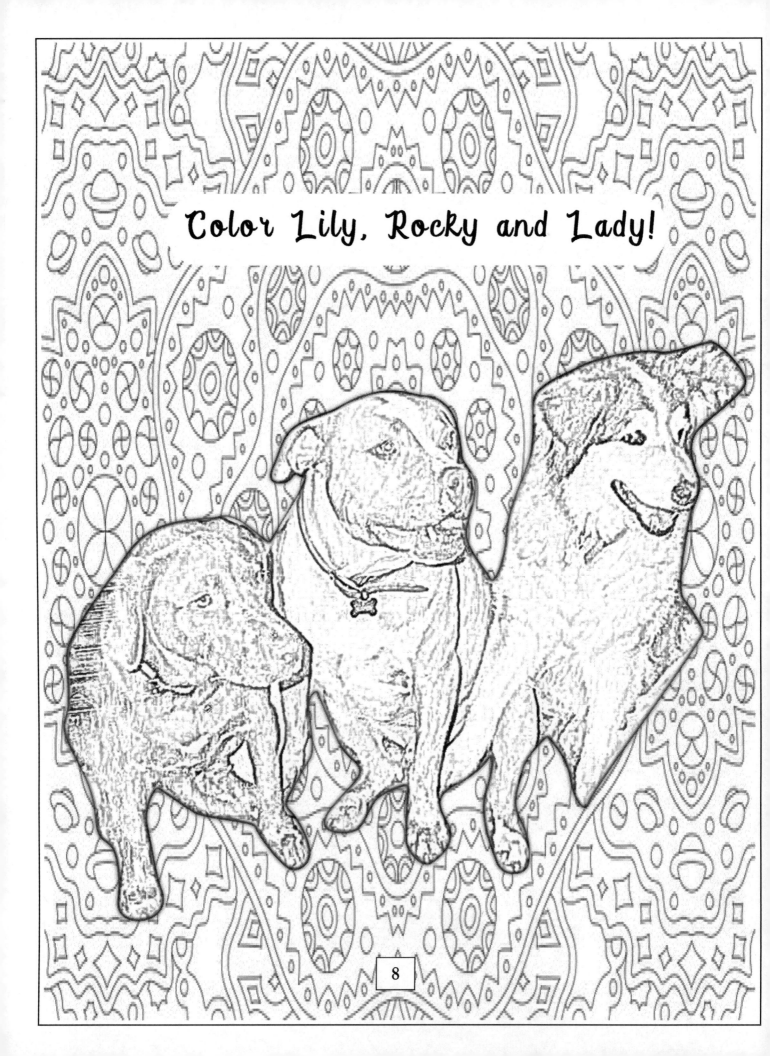

Color Lily, Rocky and Lady!

8

9

Color Spunky!

10

11

Color Baby Girl!

Color Miss Dolly Llama!

12

Color Zoie and Subie!

Color Baby Girl!

13

14

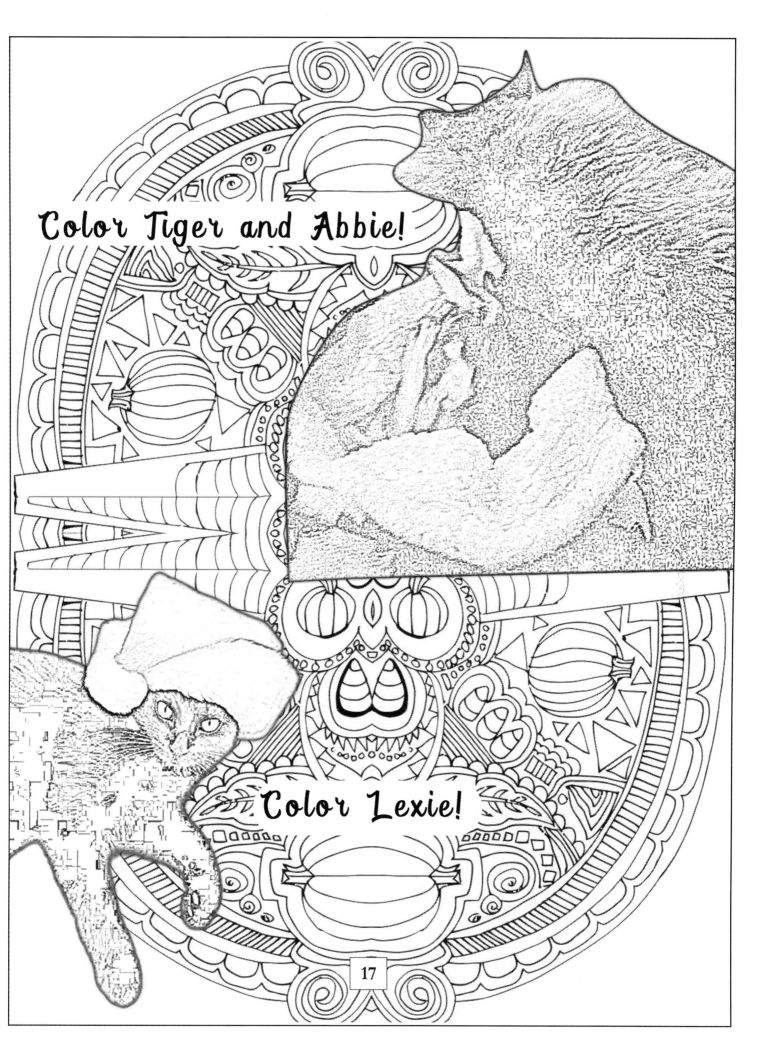

Color Tiger and Abbie!

Color Lexie!

17

Color Bear, Hazel Grace
and Macey Mae!

Color Captain America and Bucky!

Color Tessie!

20

Color Bessie and Nellie!

Color Tybear!

21

Color Sonny Dawg!

25

Color Starker Regen, Rayne Dawn and Thunder Bay!

27

28

Color Mrs. Paws and Arsle!

Color Bailey!

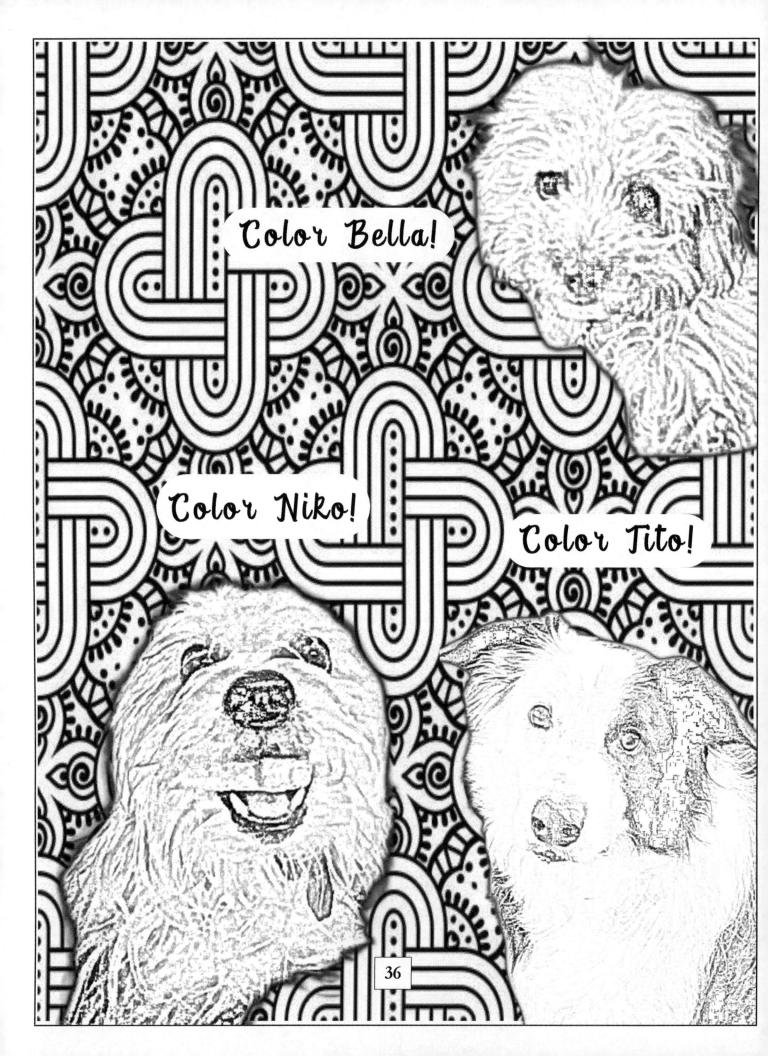

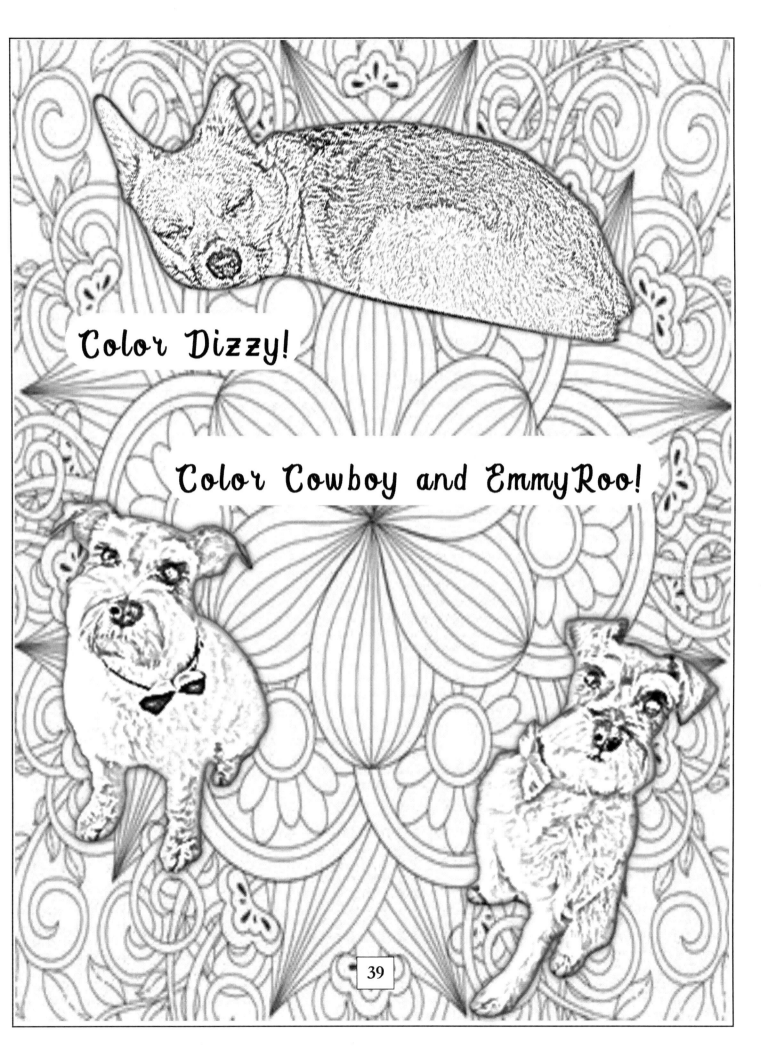

Color Dizzy!

Color Cowboy and EmmyRoo!

39

Color Sophie!

Color Bailey and Honeybunn!

40

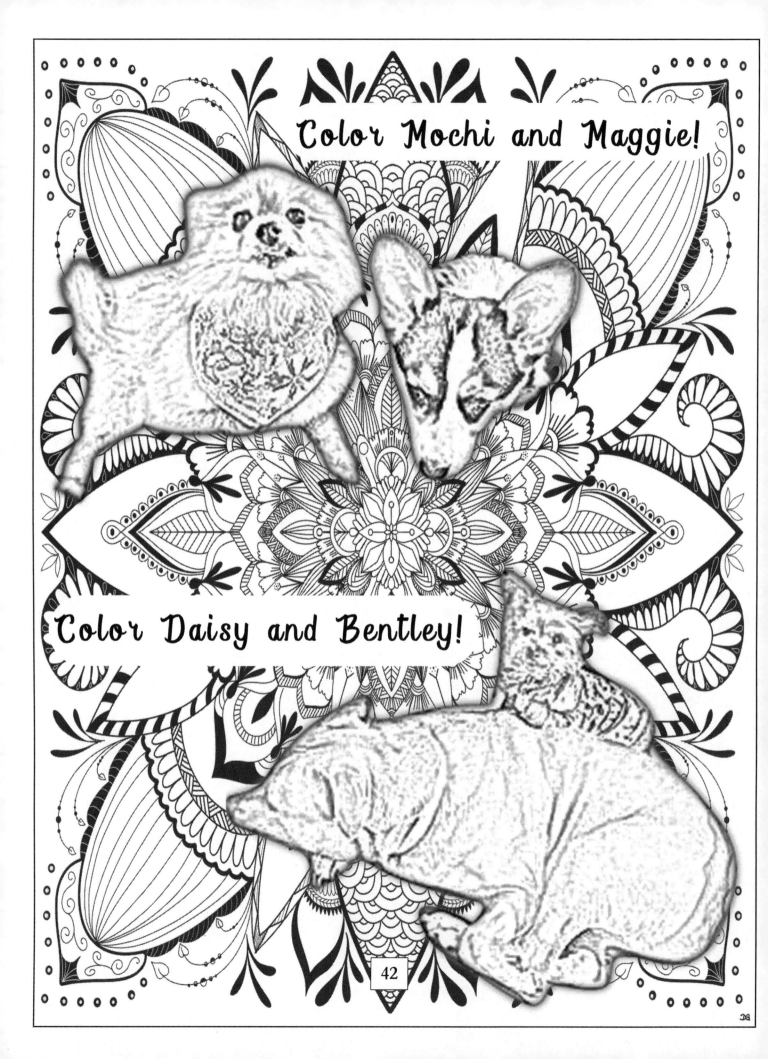

Color Mochi and Maggie!

Color Daisy and Bentley!

Color Meredith and Graywolf!

Color Cody!

44

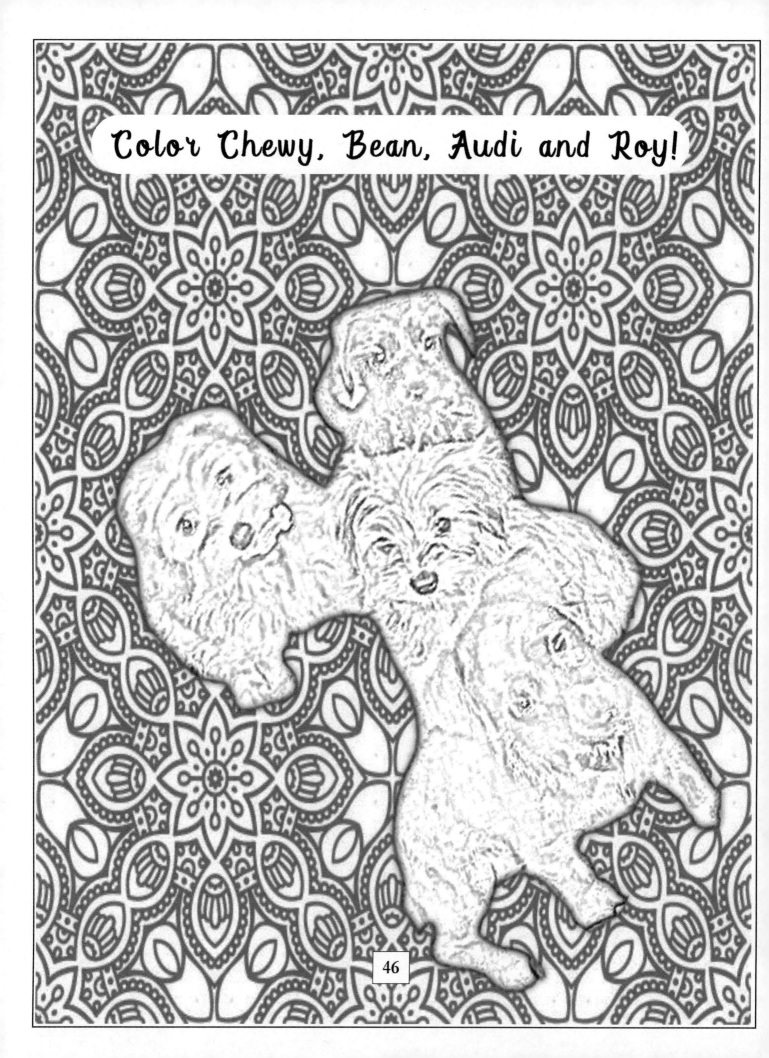

Color Chewy, Bean, Audi and Roy!

Color Willy and Waylon!

Color Zoey!

Color Sunshine!

47

Color Uso, Jaquemo, Lexi and Dakota!

51

Color Jacob and Buddy!

Color Kuechly!

54

Color Harley Rose!

Color Willow Aubrey!

Color Bella!

55

Color Bella, Zoie and Zeus!

Color Toby Teeth!

59

Color Cosmo, Ellie and Posie!

Color Cookie Monster!

Color Piper!

64

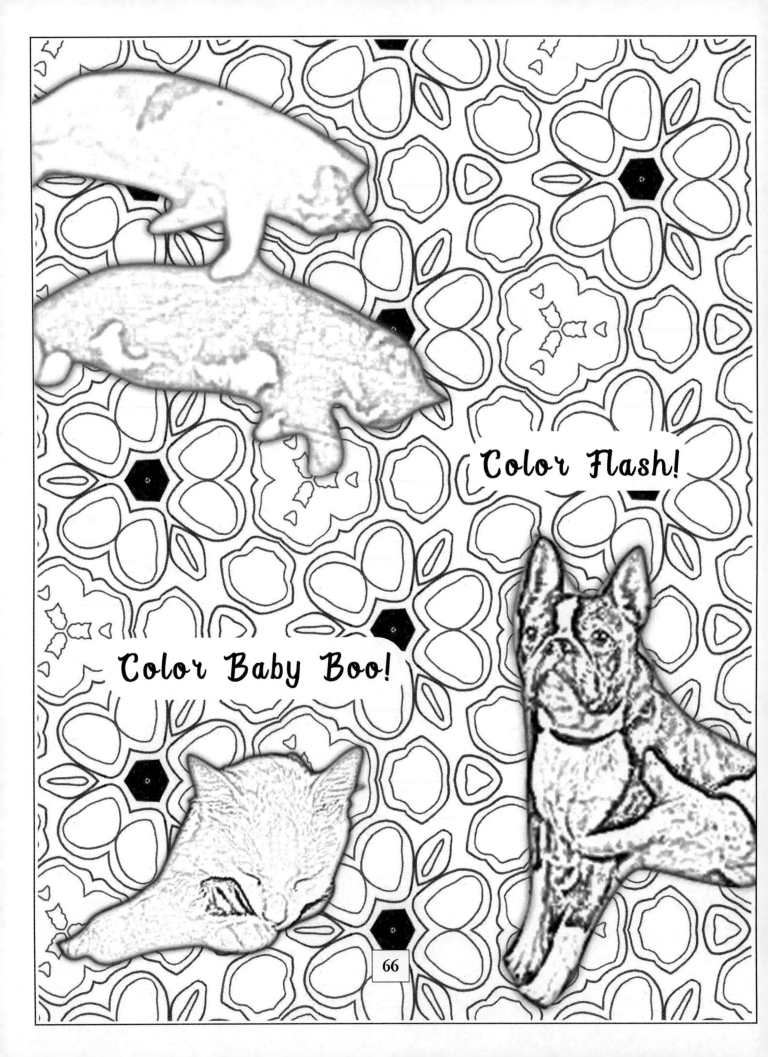

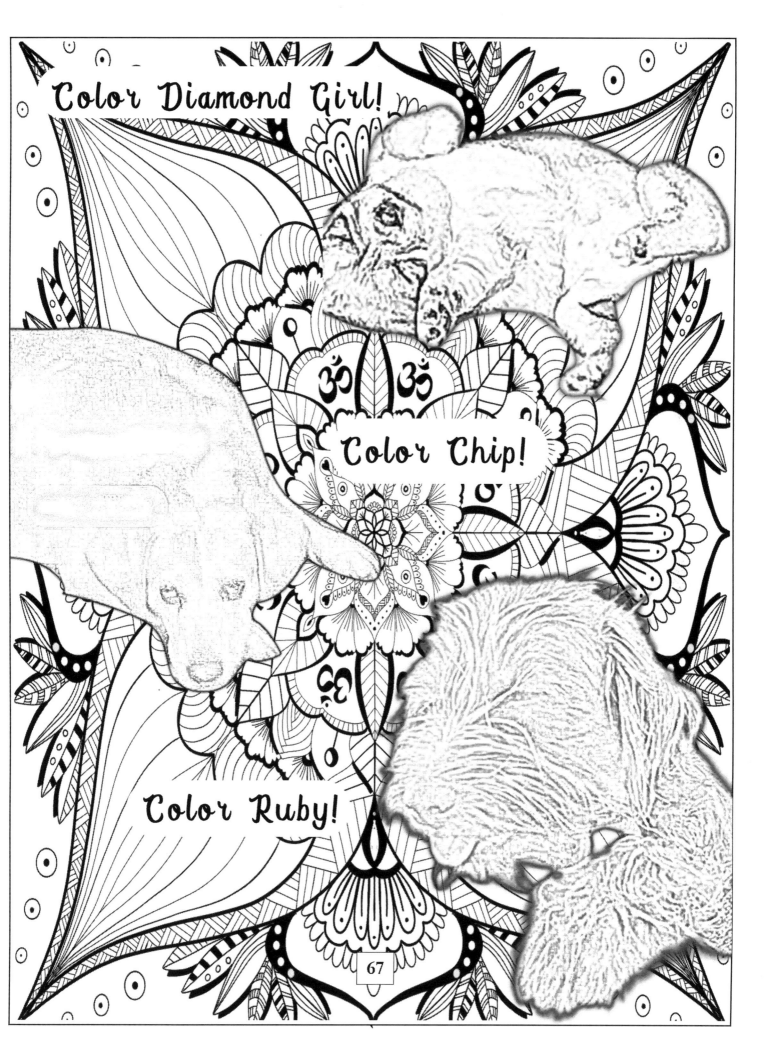

Color Diamond Girl!

Color Chip!

Color Ruby!

67

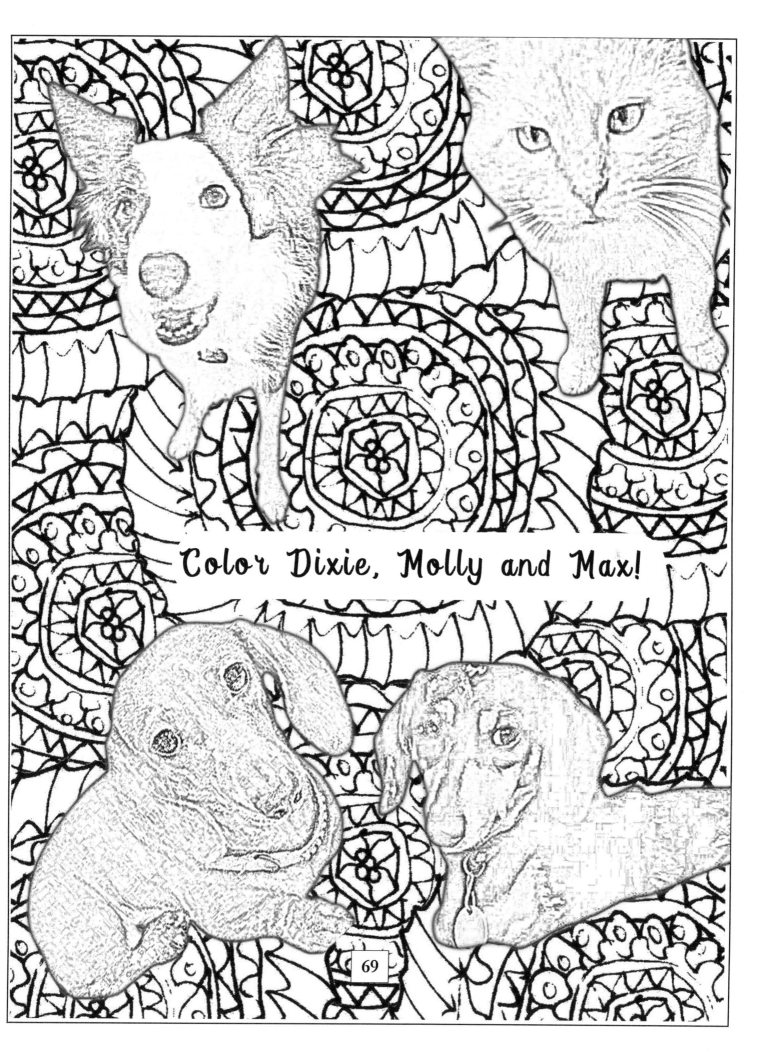

Color Dixie, Molly and Max!

69

Color Lola!

72

Color Prancer!

Color Opie!

74

Color Cowboy and Sharhhar!

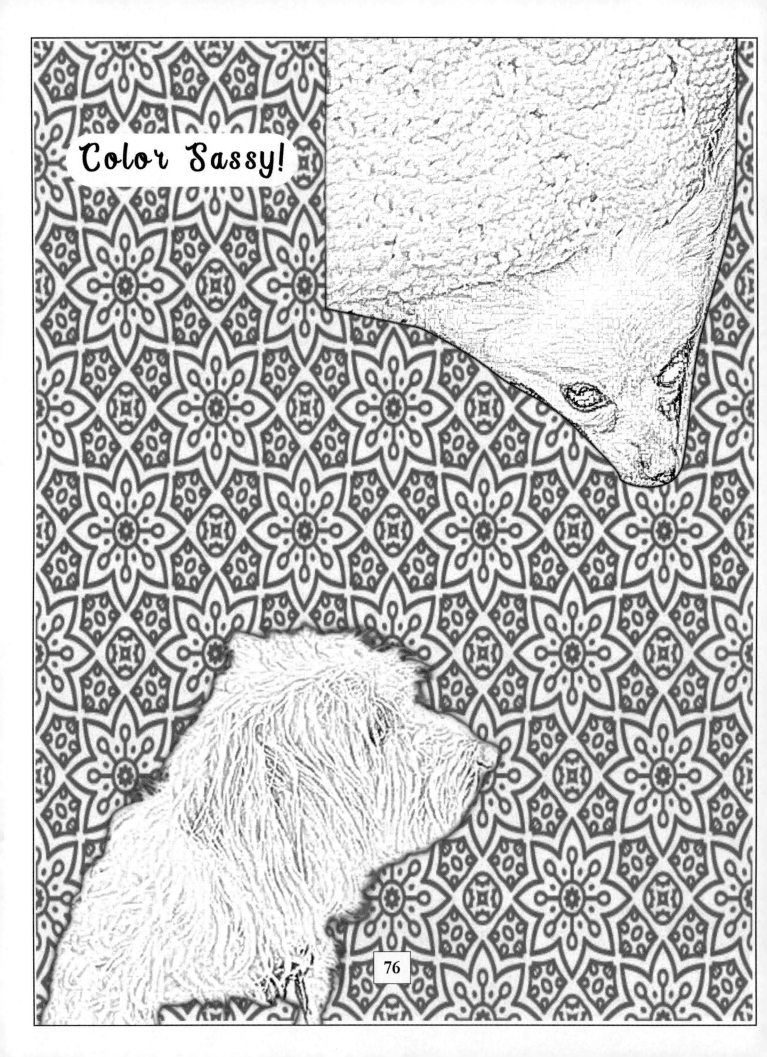

Color Bo!

Color Marshmallow!

Color Millie Mae!

78

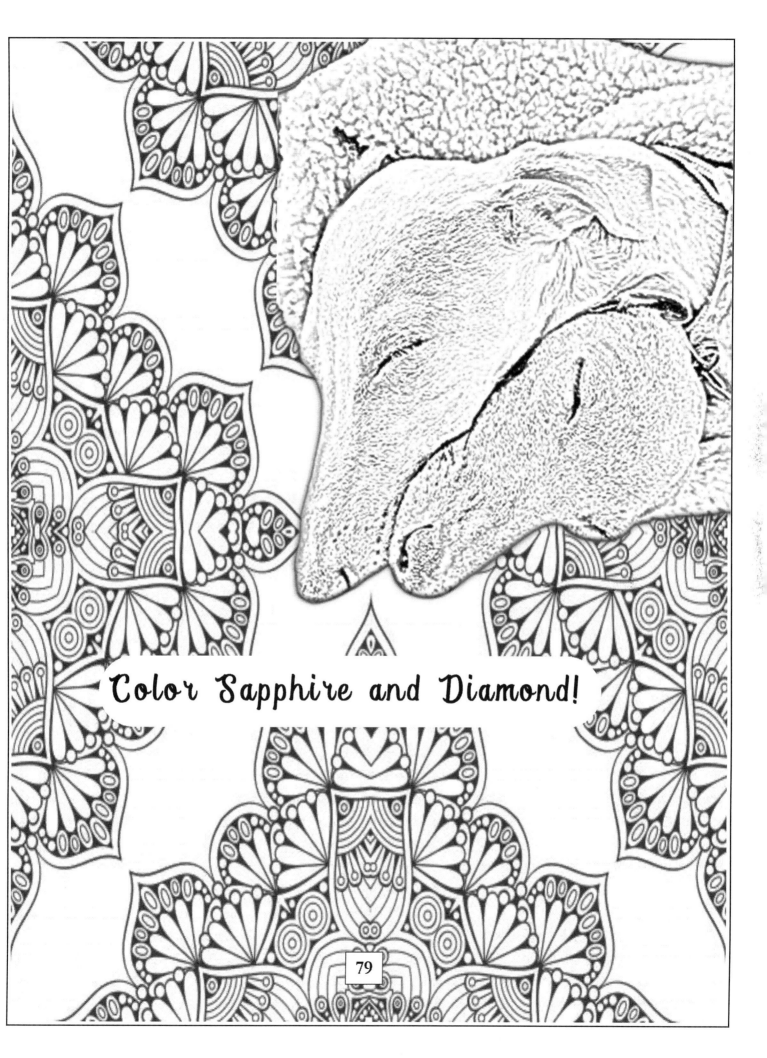

Color Sapphire and Diamond!

79

Color Marshall, Skye and Mia!

80

Color Sushi Roll, Ginger, Wasabi and Shio!

Color Cody!

83

Color Houdini and YaYa!

Color Simon!

Color Holly and Daisy!

Color Gronk!

Color Cooper!

Color Blu and Gizmo!

Color Amazing Grace!

Color Panda!

91

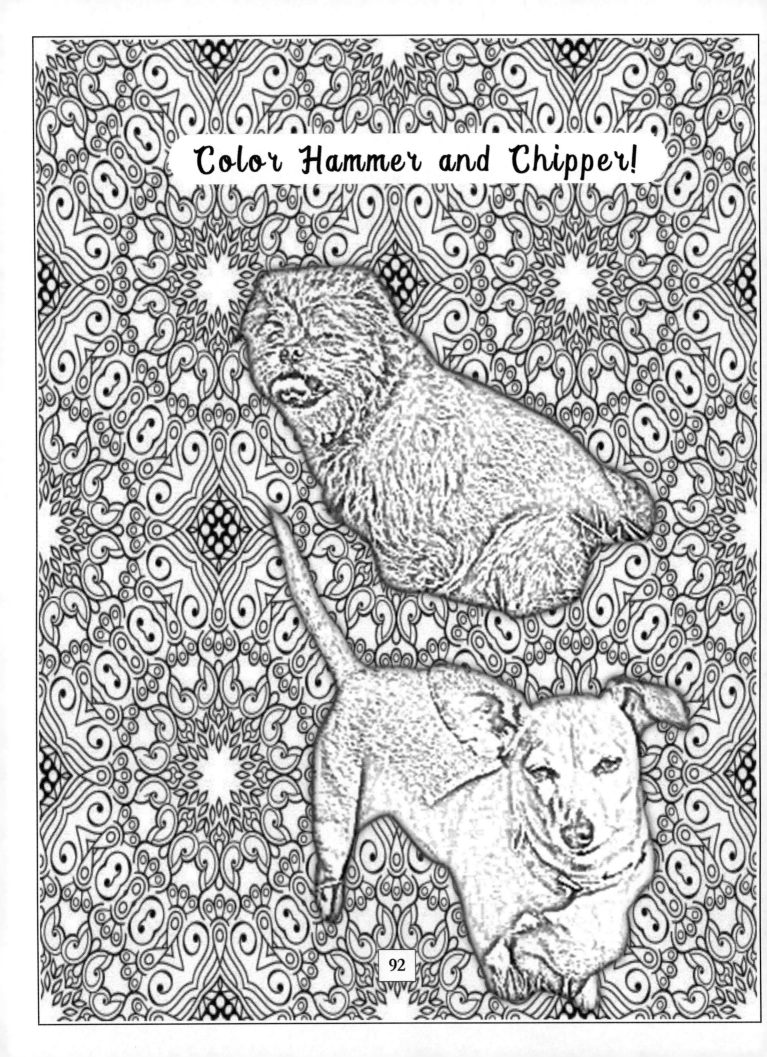

Color Hammer and Chipper!

92

Color Jersey and Harley!

Color King!

95

Color Coco!

100

Color Cabella!

Color Kuma!

102

We hope you enjoyed our coloring book! If you'd like to see YOUR pet in one of our upcoming coloring books, visit www.praisemypet.com/pages/send-us-your-pet-photos

Happy coloring!

Made in the USA
Columbia, SC
02 February 2021